I'm Going To READ!™

These levels are meant only as guides;
you and your child can best choose a book that's right.

Level 1: Kindergarten–Grade 1 . . . Ages 4–6

- word bank to highlight new words
- consistent placement of text to promote readability
- easy words and phrases
- simple sentences build to make simple stories
- art and design help new readers decode text

Level 2: Grade 1 . . . Ages 6–7

- word bank to highlight new words
- rhyming texts introduced
- more difficult words, but vocabulary is still limited
- longer sentences and longer stories
- designed for easy readability

Level 3: Grade 2 . . . Ages 7–8

- richer vocabulary of up to 200 different words
- varied sentence structure
- high-interest stories with longer plots
- designed to promote independent reading

Level 4: Grades 3 and up . . . Ages 8 and up

- richer vocabulary of more than 300 different words
- short chapters, multiple stories, or poems
- more complex plots for the newly independent reader
- emphasis on reading for meaning

LEVEL 4

Library of Congress Cataloging-in-Publication Data Available

2 4 6 8 10 9 7 5 3 1

Published by Sterling Publishing Co., Inc.
387 Park Avenue South, New York, NY 10016
Text copyright © 2005 by Harriet Ziefert Inc.
Illustrations copyright © 2005 by Amanda Haley
Distributed in Canada by Sterling Publishing
c/o Canadian Manda Group, 165 Dufferin Street
Toronto, Ontario, Canada M6K 3H6
Distributed in Great Britain and Europe by Chris Lloyd at Orca Book
Services, Stanley House, Fleets Lane, Poole BH15 3AJ, England
Distributed in Australia by Capricorn Link (Australia) Pty. Ltd.
P.O. Box 704, Windsor, NSW 2756, Australia

I'm Going To Read is a trademark of Sterling Publishing Co., Inc.

Sterling ISBN 1-4027-2084-X

PIZZA
and OTHER
STINKY POEMS

Pictures by Amanda Haley

Sterling Publishing Co., Inc.
New York

ONIONS

Onions are round
And yellow and smelly.
No one would eat them
With strawberry jelly.

But cut into rings
And fried up in batter,
I'd eat them all day
And get fatter and fatter.

LEMONADE

Lemons on parade!
Lemons on parade!
Pay me just a quarter
and I'll make you lemonade.

GOOD EVENING, MR. SOUP

Good evening, Mr. Soup, Soup, Soup,
    You taste as good as ink.

Good evening, Mr. Soup, Soup, Soup,
    You're awfully weak, we think.

Yesterday, they told me, you were Irish stew.
    Today you are back, and you taste like glue.

Good evening, Mr. Soup, Soup, Soup,

You taste about as good as . . .

You taste about as good as . . .

You taste about as good as

INK!

WHOEVER SAU-SAGE A THING?

One day a boy went walking
And strolled into a store.
He bought a pound of sausages
And laid them on the floor.

The boy began to whistle
A merry little tune,
And all the little sausages
Danced around the room!

KETCHUP

When you tip the ketchup bottle,
First will come a little, then a lot'll.

TOMATO

An accident happened
To my brother Jim
When somebody threw
A tomato at him.

Tomatoes are juicy
And don't hurt the skin,
But this one, unfortunately,
Was packed in a tin!

WATERMELON

Once my watermelon
Was nothing but a seed.
I put it in the ground
And pulled up all the weeds.

Watermelon, watermelon, on the vine.
Watermelon, watermelon, looks so fine.

First came a sprout,
Then came a vine,
Then came a flower,
And all of it was mine.

Watermelon, watermelon, on the vine.
Watermelon, watermelon, looks so fine.

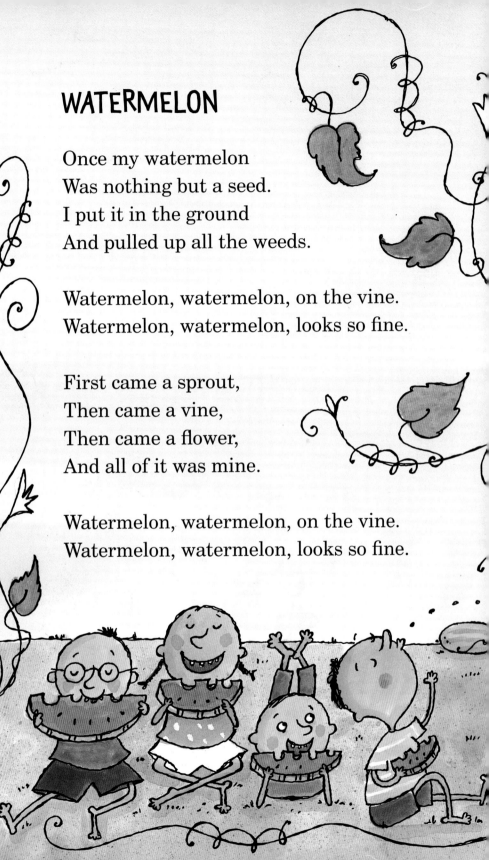

I took you to the kitchen,
Put you where it's cold,
Cut you into pieces
So you could be sold.

Watermelon, watermelon, on the vine.
Watermelon, watermelon, looks so fine.

One piece for the pony,
One piece for the pig,
Plenty for the family
Because you grew so big.
Watermelon, watermelon, on the vine.
Watermelon, watermelon, looks so fine.

FRESH FISH

You can smell
Fried fresh fish,
Fish fried fresh,
Fresh fried fish,
Fresh fish fried,
Or fish fresh fried.

However you cook it,
It smells like FISH!

STICKY BUN

Deborah Delora,
She liked a bit of fun—
She went to the baker's
And bought a great big bun.

She dipped it in molasses
And threw it at her teacher—
Deborah Delora . . .
What a wicked creature!

PEANUT BUTTER

There are three ways to get peanut butter
off the roof of your mouth.

One way is to
shake your head back  and forth.

If that doesn't work,
you could kind of whis

If that doesn't work,
you could scrape it off
with your finger.

There are three ways to get
peanut butter off your finger.

One way is to shake it off.

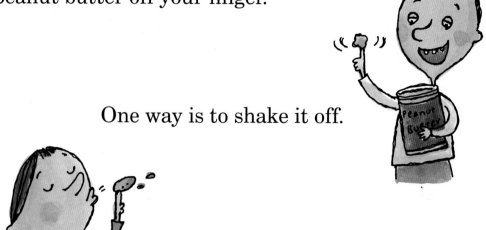

Another way is to blow it off.

If that doesn't work, you can scrape it off
with your two front teeth.

There are three ways to get peanut butter off
the roof of your mouth. . . .

MARY HAD A LITTLE LAMB

Mary had a little lamb,
A lobster and some prunes,
A glass of milk, a piece of pie,
And then some macaroons.

It made the busy waiters grin
To see her order so,
And when they carried Mary out,
Her face was white as snow.

CHOWDER CHANT

"Who put the overalls in Mrs. Murphy's chowder?"

Nobody answered, so she said it all the louder.

"Who put the overalls in Mrs. Murphy's chowder?"

Nobody answered, so she said it all the louder.

"Who put the overalls in
Mrs. Murphy's chowder?"

Nobody answered, so she said it all the louder.

"Who put the overalls in Mrs. Murphy's chowder?"

Hey, what kind of chowder is this anyway?

LITTLE MISS MUFFET

Little Miss Muffet sat on a tuffet,
Eating her curds and whey.
Along came a spider who sat down beside her
And said,

PIZZA

Through the teeth
And past the gums
Look out stomach,
Pizza comes.

POTATO CHIPS

Charlie Chomp is munching chips.
  Salt and vinegar, salt and vinegar.
Charlie Chomp has munched them.

Charlie Chomp is munching chips.
  Really salted, really salted.
  Salt and vinegar, salt and vinegar.
Charlie Chomp has munched them.

Charlie Chomp is feeling sick.
Charlie has a bellyache and . . . ICK!

RAVIOLI

Ravioli, yummy ravioli—
Ravioli, that's the stuff for me.
Do you have it on your sleeve?
Yes, I have it on my sleeve?
On your sleeve?
On my sleeve.
Ravioli, yummy ravioli—
Ravioli, that's the stuff for me.

Do you have it on your pants?

Do you have it on your shoe?

MEATBALL

On top of spaghetti
All covered with cheese,
I lost my poor meatball
When somebody sneezed.

It rolled off the table
And onto the floor.
Then my poor meatball
Rolled out the door.

It rolled into the garden
And under a bush,
And then my poor meatball
Was nothing but mush.

But the mush was so tasty,
As tasty can be.
Early last summer
It grew into a tree.

The tree was all covered
With beautiful moss
And grew lots of meatballs
In to-mato sauce.

So when you eat spaghetti
All covered with cheese,
Hang onto your meatball
And don't ever sneeze!

STEW

When I found a mouse in my stew,
I raised a great hullabaloo.
"Please don't shout," the waiter said,
"Or the others will want one too!"

PIE

Oh my,
I want a piece of pie.

The pie's too sweet,
I want a piece of meat.

The meat's too red,
I want a piece of bread.

The bread's too brown,
I'd better go to town.

The town's too far,
I need a trolley car.

The car's too slow,
I fell and stubbed my toe.

My toe's got a pain,
I'd better take a train.

The train had a wreck,
I nearly broke my neck.

Oh my, no more pie.

ICE CREAM

I scream,
You scream,
We all scream
For ice cream!

BURP

Better to urp a burp
And bear the shame,
Than squelch a belch
And die of pain.

FULL

Here I stand all fat and chunky.
Ate a duck and swallowed a donkey!

SHOW-AND-SMELL

I found an apple.
It was rotten.
I put it where
It wouldn't be forgotten.

A few days later
My teacher said, "Nell,
Now it's your turn
For show-and-tell."

I didn't have anything
For show-and-tell . . .
But I did have an apple
For show-and-smell!